ideals®
MOTHER'S DAY

More Than 50 Years of Celebrating Life's Most Treasured Moments

Vol. 54, No. 2

"The cornerstone of every home,
The most important part,
Is never laid upon the earth
But in a mother's heart."

—*Lydia O. Jackson*

IDEALS—Vol. 54, No. 2 March MCMXCVII IDEALS (ISSN 0019-137X) is published six times a year: January, March,
May, July, September, and November by IDEALS PUBLICATIONS INCORPORATED,
535 Metroplex Drive, Suite 250, Nashville, TN 37211.
Periodical postage paid at Nashville, Tennessee, and additional mailing offices.
Copyright © MCMXCVII by IDEALS PUBLICATIONS INCORPORATED.
POSTMASTER: Send address changes to Ideals, PO Box 305300, Nashville, TN 37230. All rights reserved.
Title IDEALS registered U.S. Patent Office.

SINGLE ISSUE—U.S. $5.95 USD; Higher in Canada
ONE-YEAR SUBSCRIPTION—U.S. $19.95 USD; Canada $36.00 CDN (incl. GST and shipping); Foreign $25.95 USD
TWO-YEAR SUBSCRIPTION—U.S. $35.95 USD; Canada $66.50 CDN (incl. GST and shipping); Foreign $47.95 USD

The cover and entire contents of IDEALS are fully protected by copyright and must not be reproduced in any manner whatsoever.

Printed and bound in USA by Quebecor Printing. Printed on Weyerhaeuser Husky.

The paper used in this publication meets the minimum requirements of
American National Standard for Information Sciences—
Permanence of Paper for Printed Library Materials, ANSI Z39.48-1984.

Subscribers may call customer service at 1-800-558-4343 to make address changes.
Unsolicited manuscripts will not be returned without a self-addressed, stamped envelope.

ISBN 0-8249-1142-3   GST 131903775

Cover Photo
HYDRANGEA BOUQUET
H. Armstrong Roberts

Inside Covers
GARDEN VIEW, JUNE MORNING
Charles Neal, artist

MORNING

James Whitcomb Riley

Breath of morning, breath of May,
  With your zest of yesterday
And crisp, balmy freshness, smite
  Our old hearts with youth's delight.

Tilt the cap of boyhood, yea,
  Where no forelock waves, today—
Back, in breezy, cool excess,
  Stroke it with the old caress.

Let us see as we have seen,
  Where all paths are dewy-green
And all humankind are kin—
  Let us be as we have been!

PRING

George R. Kossik

Spring will sprout,
The blossoms will show forth their bloom,
And on some sweet-scented bough,
Half dazed with delights of perfume,
The red-breasted robin will sing
In praise of the glorious spring.

GARDEN WALL
Phoenix, Arizona
Dick Dietrich Photography

SPRINGTIME PRAYER

Carice Williams

We thank you, God, for spring's return,
   For joy that sweet May brings,
For miracles occurring now
   In all earth's growing things.
For length'ning days, for sunshine's warmth
   Our grateful hearts will sing
Because once more You gave to us
   Another wondrous spring.

DAYS OF SPRING

Nora M. Bozeman

Spring in urgent infancy
   Hangs apple blossoms on a tree,
Paints gold on dainty daffodils,
   Flings verdant green on sleeping hills.

Spring adorned in artistry
   Spreads cloud ballets from sea to sea,
Spills sunsets from a crimson jar,
   Then sleeps upon a silvered star.

THE BREEZE AND I

John W. Williams

I walk at twilight cross the farm
And feel her hand upon my arm,
My unseen date, the evening breeze,
Who wears cologne of apple trees.

But soon she finds another swain
And strokes the hair of fields of grain.
As she goes skipping on the lake,
A rippled smile lies in her wake.

The lonesome pine, the balsam fir,
All nature seems in awe of her.
While further flaunting all her charms,
She waltzes in the willow's arms.

Though she is fickle as can be,
Caressing every weed and tree,
I still return again to seek
Her fleeting kiss against my cheek.

4

Kentucky, Wait!

Stella Craft Tremble

Kentucky, wait! I'm coming home
 To see the daffodils,
Where dogwood drops its satin blooms
 Upon the hazy hills,

Where sheaves of water on a rock
 Fall on a wind-bent tree,
Where light and shadow flicker on
 In golden harmony.

I'll feel the playful breezes blow
 A fragrance from the pine
That clings upon the ridge's crest
 Against the timberline.

I'll see the sky-dome sagging
 With constellation strain,
Be lulled to peaceful slumber
 By the pattering of rain.

Kentucky, wait! I'm coming home
 To see such things as these.
No other place does springtime have
 Such magic certainties.

May Baskets

Freda V. Fisher

We used to hang baskets
The first day of May
On somebody's doorknob
And then run away.

We'd hide and watch someone
Come open the door
And search the whole street.
Who were they looking for?

We'd giggle and chuckle
As we heard them say,

"Now who left me flowers?"
Then we'd run and play.

The flowers were wild,
Whatever we'd find.
Yellow dandelions mostly,
But moms never mind.

To us they were priceless,
Gold gems from above.
To our moms who received them,
They were baskets of love.

May Day

Mamie Ozburn Odum

I stood upon the hill and watched the dawn
Replace the star-crowned brow of fading night;
I heard the soft winds' tuneful symphony,
Saw diamond dewdrops fill the sun-kissed light.
The silver clouds sailed high above the earth.
I stood and saw God paint the morning sky,
Saw little homes content in green below,
Saw children with schoolbooks go romping by.

I saw a farmer with his faithful mules;
A spotless line of clothes danced in the breeze,
A church spire's beauty met the sloping hill,
And birds sang anthems from the aging trees.
Heavenly splendor graced the springlike day;
For Spring had come, her baskets filled with May.

Readers' Reflections

Editor's Note: Readers are invited to submit unpublished, original poetry for possible publication in future issues of Ideals. *Please send typed copies only; manuscripts will not be returned. Writers receive $10 for each published submission. Send material to Readers' Reflections, Ideals Publications Inc., 535 Metroplex Drive, Suite 250, Nashville, Tennessee 37211.*

REMEMBERING MOTHER

Of all the words, there is no other
More dear to me than the word mother.
For mother means so many things,
Revealing all the love it brings.
It starts a joy down in my heart
From which I never could depart.
Her lovely eyes would seem to glow.
And with a smile, she'd always know
Before I'd even say a word
As if with inner voice she heard
What I was thinking; but she'd wait
To show me if I'd hesitate,

I'd need not fear, that she'd be glad
To share my secrets, good or bad!
She knew she'd taught me right from wrong,
That trusting God would keep me strong.
Her faith showed in the prayers she said,
Learned from the Bible, daily read.
The stories she so often told
Meant more to me than gifts of gold.
Her special sense of humor too
She shared when I was feeling blue.
I'm thankful for each memory
My precious mother gave to me!

Margaret Umland
Clinton, Indiana

NEW BABY

You sit there by his cradle bed
   And watch him as he sleeps.
And you are filled with joy untold
   And your love goes oh so deep!
Your heart is filled with wonder
   At this miracle you see,
And your head holds a thousand
   Pictures of what is yet to be.
His father too is full of dreams
   Of what is yet to come,
And he just bursts with pride and joy
   As he looks at his little son.
Of all the miracles of God,
   This one is surely best,
This tiny, precious little son
   With whom you have been blessed.

Karlynn Curfman
La Selva Beh, California

FLASHBACK

She sits there like a vision
   As she smiles up at me,
A little girl from long ago
   Now here on my knee.
Child of the past or present,
   Is it now or yesterday?
She looks so like another;
   The years just fade away.
We play the games of childhood,
   We sing old songs again,
And lessons long since finished
   She's ready to begin.
My youth she brings back daily,
   Restores fond memories.
Grandparents know the blessing
   Of déjà vu, you see.

Benna Boutty
Geneva, Florida

MAY TREASURE

Though rich or poor or in between
   Whichever we may be,
The month of May pours out her wealth
   For all of us to see.
The finest silk cannot compare
   With lovely iris bloom,
And costly fragrance can't surpass
   The lilac's rich perfume.
The tulips glow like rubies;
   Fresh new leaves are emerald green;

The golden maple blossoms
   Add bright beauty to the scene.
The violets shine like purple gems
   When wet with morning dew;
Azaleas glow like radiant jewels
   Of many a glorious hue.
The birdsongs make a symphony
   That we are free to hear;
So May reveals her finest gifts
   With every passing year.

Elsie Heimroth Moger
Patchogue, New York

Harbingers of Spring

Elisabeth Weaver Winstead

I love the Maytime days of spring,
    The rippling raindrops' ting-a-ling,
The drowsy hum of gold-flecked bees
    Above the silvered cherry trees.

White hyacinths are sparkling bright;
    They lift their petals to the light.
The fragrance of spring's fresh perfume
    Drifts from the lilacs in full bloom.

Young robins in bright crimson vests
    Are here to build new family nests;

The whisp'ring trees in velvet sheen
    Hold leaves of iridescent green.

Gold tulips sway in sprightly grace
    Beside the bluebell's satin face;
Cream-colored jonquils line the walk
    By willows where small sparrows talk.

Pale butterflies in rainbow glow
    Glide o'er each shimm'ring rose below.
In soaring waves of spring's rebirth,
    Sweet May's enchantment sweeps the earth.

A New Note

Patience Strong

There's a new note in the choirs that sing
　　Upon the leafless boughs.
There's a new song in the air today,
　　A song that seems to rouse
And resurrect the life within,
　　Grown cold in winter hours,
Waking all the old, sweet dreams
　　Of blossom, buds, and flowers.

There's a new hope in the world today
　　Because of this glad sound.
There's an urgent and an upward thrust
　　Of green things in the ground.
There's a new joy in the hearts of men
　　Because of this strange note:
This rapturous reveille
　　From some little, feathered throat.

Country CHRONICLE

—Lansing Christman—

THREE BEAUTIES OF MAY

Nature always shares the beauties of May in the world of wildflowers. I doubt that she pits the loveliness of one bloom against another, for all are equal to her. And along the roadsides and in the fields right now is a splendid array of flowers, each with its own exquisite charm. But to me, three blossoms predominate the vivid color scheme in the late spring—Queen Anne's lace, the lily, and the butterfly weed. All are in flower during these lovely days of May. I cherish their beauty and their colorful arrangement of white, yellow, and orange.

Of course, I have always thought of the delicate Queen Anne's lace as a queen; I still do. The loveliness of Queen Anne's lace comes from those flat flower clusters which form an intricate lacelike pattern during the long blossoming period from May into October and beyond.

The day lily, a garden escape, comes into bloom in a burst of glory. Some of the roadsides are masses of blossoms, their brilliant colors ranging from yellow to orange. When I see the first lily of May, I always turn to the book of St. Matthew for these poetic lines: "And why take ye thought for raiment? Consider the lilies of the field, how they grow; they toil not, neither do they spin: and yet I say unto you, That even Solomon in all his glory was not arrayed like one of these" (Matthew 6:28, 29).

The humble butterfly weed is the final member of this colorful trio. The deep reddish-orange hue of the blossom glows like the burning embers of a woodfire in the kitchen stove at eventide.

Color, beauty, loveliness—each May, Queen Anne's lace, the day lily, and the butterfly weed weave a gracious garland of wildflowers across the roadsides that wind up and down through our valleys and hills.

The author of two published books, Lansing Christman has been contributing to Ideals *for more than twenty years. Mr. Christman has also been published in several American, foreign, and braille anthologies. He lives in rural South Carolina.*

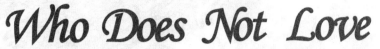

Who Does Not Love

True Poetry

Henry Clay Hall

Who does not love true poetry,
He lacks a bosom friend
　　To walk with him
　　And talk with him
And all his steps attend.

Who does not love true poetry—
Its rhythmic throb and swing,
　　The treat of it,
　　The sweet of it,
Along the paths of spring;

Its joyous lilting melody
In every passing breeze,
　　The deep of it,
　　The sweep of it,
Through hours of toil or ease;

Its grandeur and sublimity,
Its majesty and might,
　　The feel of it,
　　The peal of it,
Through all the lonely night;

Its tenderness and soothing touch;
Like balm on evening air,
　　That feelingly
　　And healingly
Cures all the hurts of care.

Who does not love true poetry
Of sea and sky and sod—
　　The height of it
　　The might of it—
He has not known his God.

From My Garden Journal

by Deana Deck

WISTERIA

I've finally given in. After years of fending off temptation, I've succumbed at last. Oh, I had heard all the stories. I had heard about gutters and shingles and shutters that had to be pried off homes. I had heard about attics invaded, chimneys cast asunder, and trellises crushed to splinters. All that, of course, was before Savannah, before I saw them in their full glory. Before I surrendered and planted my very own wisteria.

As a lover of lilacs, I had convinced myself that I could live a happy life without wisteria because—based on color and fragrance—lilacs were an acceptable substitute. From all I'd heard, wisteria was nothing but trouble. For example, wisteria can take from six to nine years to bloom, and for most of my life I had never lived in one place long enough to even consider that sort of commitment. But, like I said, that was before Savannah.

A couple of years ago, in early spring, a friend and I tied our bicycles on top of my station wagon and headed south for a long weekend. Our trip coincided with Savannah's Old Town Garden Tours, and we visited every garden we could. On one of the many parklike squares for which Savannah is famous, there was a home that had an ancient live oak tree that appeared to be dripping purple blooms. Only when I noticed the huge, gnarled vine twining up the tree's trunk did I realize I was seeing my first mature wisteria. It was spectacular.

The vine reached to the top of the trunk and branched out in all directions, winding its way through the leafy canopy in search of sunlight. Along the way, it draped massive panicles of lavender-blue blossoms down through the branches. The longer I stood there staring at it, the more I realized I was doomed. I had to have one of my own. I was determined, however, to avoid the pitfalls I had heard so much about.

One of my assumptions about wisteria was put to rest on that same trip. On the drive home I noticed wisteria growing wild along the interstate. It was in full bloom, which squelched rumors about the plant's requirement for excessive care. I was becoming even more attracted, although I had not yet abandoned all my reservations.

Another misconception I had was that the wisteria was too tender to thrive in temperate climates. That was disproved a week or so later when I noticed yet another highway-cruising wisteria. This one was draped over the sound-barrier walls that enclose a section of interstate in my own hometown, two climate zones north of Savannah.

My horticultural encyclopedia revealed

WISTERIA

that not only is wisteria hardy in the Zone 6 climate of the mid-South, it is hardy clear up to Zone 4—which translates into Maine, Minnesota, and Montana, for example.

I also discovered why wisteria and interstates were becoming intertwined. Since wisteria is resistant to pollution, it has become a popular landscaping choice along highways, especially urban routes bound by high walls.

Several species of wisteria exist, but the most widely planted are the Japanese (*Wisteria floribunda*) and the Chinese (*W. sinensis*). Both are hardy and fast growing, and both require the same care and soil conditions. The difference is that the Japanese wisteria is more fragrant and blooms gradually, with flower clusters that open first at the base and progress toward the tip. The Chinese wisteria is less fragrant, but puts on a more spectacular show, with the entire cluster blooming all at once.

I've known about the wisteria's penchant for being a late bloomer for years. One reason is that wisterias grown from seeds do not flower well and often not until they are twenty or more years old. Purchase your plant from a reputable garden center and be sure it was grown from rooted cuttings. Also, wisteria grown in the north is more susceptible to late frosts that can damage buds. Another factor is that wisteria just takes time getting a strong root system established. To get your plants off to a good start, dig a deep planting hole and amend it generously with compost and rich loam. Add bone meal and composted manure. Use nitrogen sparingly, and, if your soil is heavy, add sand to encourage good drainage. The soil should be moist, but not wet. Plant the vines in full sun, as they do not bloom well in shade. If wisteria is planted under trees and does bloom, you will lose sight of the flowers because the vine will head for the sky in search of sunlight, taking the blossoms with it.

Let the young plant get a good start for about three years, watering and feeding regularly, but without expecting blooms. During this time, train the vine along wires, a pergola, or some other strong support. Be advised, however, to plant your wisteria away from your house in order to protect your gutters, eaves, and even your attic from intruding vines.

A word of warning is in order if you have small children: the seed pods of wisteria are quite attractive, but the seeds, which resemble beans, are highly poisonous.

My wisteria was a three-foot tall container plant when I bought it. By last fall it had wound itself to the top of an eight-foot locust pole that I secured to the side of a hackberry tree. Once I realized how fast it was growing, I rounded up some ten-foot cedar poles and designed a permanent trellis.

I am no longer a wisteria-resister. I confess that I have been won over and now find myself dreaming about one day serving springtime lunch to friends under a shady canopy of fragrant wisteria blooms. Until then, I'll make do with a centerpiece of lilacs.

Deana Deck tends to her flowers, plants, and vegetables at her home in Nashville, Tennessee, where her popular garden column is a regular feature in The Tennessean.

Apart

Marie Hunter Dawson

I like to go in the morning
　　When the blossoms are dripping dew
Into the heart of my garden room
　　And work for an hour or two.
The air is laden with perfume,
　　And the paint on the flowers is wet.
For the sun is young and the air is cool;
　　Not a petal has withered yet.

I like to loosen up the earth
　　Around the tender shoots
To let the stream from quenching showers
　　Seep through to thirsty roots.
I hear a chorus of birds and breeze
　　As I kneel on the mellow sod
And hold in fragrance and beauty and song
　　A morning communion with God.

These beautiful days most
enrich all my life. They do
not exist as mere pictures—
maps hung upon the walls of
memory . . . but they saturate
themselves into every part
of the body and live always.

　　　　　　—John Muir

TRAVELER'S Diary

Nancy Skarmeas

THE NATCHEZ TRACE PARKWAY
Tennessee to Mississippi

Between Natchez, Mississippi, and Nashville, Tennessee, runs the Natchez Trace Parkway—a truly beautiful stretch of road. The Trace, as it is known, is actually thousands of years old: it began as a series of buffalo trails and Native American footpaths leading away from the Mississippi River, through dense forests and toward the more open areas to the northeast. When European settlers arrived in the area, they took advantage of this ready-made path to travel in the opposite direction, moving further and further south in search of fertile land. Through the years, some of the great names in American history made use of this route: Meriwether Lewis, Andrew Jackson, John J. Audubon, and the legendary Shawnee chief Tecumseh are all part of the rich history of the Trace; as were countless ordinary men and women—settlers, soldiers, entrepreneurs, missionaries, and more—who made their way south along this ancient highway. By the turn of the nineteenth century, the Trace had become one of the most traveled routes in the United States; only a decade later, however, it became obsolete. In 1807, the invention of the steamboat revolutionized travel on the great Mississippi River. It was not long before the Natchez Trace seemed a tedious way to travel.

I spent the last few days traveling this historic road, which is now maintained by the National Park Service. Off limits to billboard advertising and to commercial traffic, the Natchez Trace is today a long, narrow oasis of colorful history and lovely southern landscapes. Along the route are historical markers, picnic areas, nature trails, and a string of charming old inns that once served weary travelers arriving on foot or on horseback. The terrain is ever-changing: the Mississippi River; the thick forests, lush and green with springtime vegetation; the endless array of flowers in bloom along crystal clear streams; the wide, open fields, where I saw wild turkey alongside white-tailed deer; the stately oaks, draped gracefully with moss; the giant, towering old pine trees; and the cypress swamps, alive with the sounds of springtime in the deep South. Along the unspoiled route of the Trace, it was not impossible to imagine that what I saw was little changed from the natural world that greeted settlers as they walked this route two centuries before me.

Almost two hundred years ago, when our nation was growing by leaps and bounds, when progress was the word on everyone's lips, the timeworn Natchez Trace was abandoned to the pages of history. Age has brought us wisdom, however, and an understanding of the value of our heritage. For many of us, myself included, on a lovely spring day in the warm southern sunshine, progress and speed and the future are not as appealing as peace and quiet and history. Thank goodness for the steamboats that left this road frozen in time and for the careful custodians of history who have sheltered it from progress and development! On one of the many nature trails along the Trace, a marker invites the visitor not only to learn the history of the Trace, but to become a part of it: "Walk down the shaded trail and leave your prints in the dust," it reads, "not for others to see, but for the road to remember." I left my prints on the Natchez Trace; whether the road will truly remember I cannot say, but I know for certain that I will not soon forget.

A Mother's Tears, A Mother's Smile

John C. Bonser

When I was born, at first I cried
And flailed my small limbs side to side
Until my mother's safe arms kept
Me close beside her and I slept;

While gazing on her newborn child,
Through tears of joy my mother smiled.

The night I wed my lovely bride,
Holding her with heartfelt pride,
We marched back up the festooned aisle
And everywhere saw people smile;

But, almost hidden at one side,
My mother watched and softly cried.

The other day, dear Mother died.
And kneeling by her stricken side,
I held her hand and, helpless, wept,
For now she was the one who slept;

And I could not give her new life
Within this womb of earthly strife

Nor walk beside her to that place
Where love lives on with angel-grace.
Yet from that place I seem to see
My mother, still, smile down at me!

26

Remember When

MY GRANDMOTHER'S GARDEN
Carol Bessent Hayman

A garden begins quietly, as do many things of great significance in our lives. It is part of all our childhood hopes and longings—a green place in which to dream and play. Beginning in the mind and the heart, a garden's silence beckons with enchantment. It is part of the music of the earth—trees move in the breeze, birds call and reply, an ancient mystery passes through and touches all.

Whether their garden is a bloom-covered acre or a tiny porch filled with robust containers, all gardeners enjoy the out-of-doors. They take it like nourishment, which indeed it is to the soul of a gardener. It has never surprised me that, wherever I lived, I always had a garden. Sometimes it was only a few rows of zinnias or tomatoes, and sometimes I stayed long enough to plant roses and fruit trees. The urge was deep inside me, twined around memories of my grandmother. Even her name, Rose, evokes images of a garden.

In my mind I can see her patiently watering her blooming yard, tending her geraniums and begonias, coaxing her old-fashioned yellow rose on our backyard trellis and accepting compliments on her fragrant gardenias. Watching her, I learned to love the land. As the oldest grandchild, I became her helper, her errand girl, and almost her shadow. Her influence is felt in many areas of my life and, importantly, in my love of gardens. I live on the piece of land she knew and cultivated, in the house she dreamed of long before my grandfather built it for her. I am part of the town where she was born, married, and lived her life. Familiar things, shared thoughts, and warm memories surround me, and nowhere more than in my yard and garden.

Still, my yard today is a testament to change. Where my grandmother had what she called a "wood house" (for storing firewood), I have a gazebo; where her trellised yellow rose grew, I have an ivy-covered brick wall; where she raised chickens and pumped water, my pink and white oleanders flourish as tall as the dogwood which shades the swing. My flagstone walkways follow my memories of her worn paths, the paths I walked with her so many times in my childhood.

The entrances to the yard and garden remain where they have always been; however, I have added a stone birdbath, and small pieces of statuary now dot the lawn along with a Victorian gazing ball. Lanterns light the night and give safe passage to and from a quiet, grassy nook with a welcoming bench. And enclosing it all is a sturdy, white picket fence in an almost lacy pattern.

Evenings often find me quietly enjoying the sights and scents of my garden, where I remember moonlit nights when I sat with my grandmother on the porch overlooking the yard and rocked to the rhythm of those dear surroundings. We spoke love's language, which is to read each other's thoughts and answer with soft words such as "of course," "always," and "yes, tomorrow."

I am alone (as she never was) on this land, and yet the porches hold me; the yard and garden sustain and comfort me. At evening, as shadows fall, I can see her among the flower beds, and I understand, quietly, the words, "Welcome to my garden."

GARDEN OF MEMORIES

Edith Roscoe Hilsinger

Grandmother's garden smelled of phlox,
Forget-me-nots, and four-o'clocks.
Morning-glories, heavenly blue,
Climbed the rustic fence to view
Grandmother and her shadow, me—
The little girl that used to be.
"Flowers talk," one day she said,
Pausing by the pansy bed.
"Pansies are for thoughts, you see.
Roses, for love." Then, tenderly,
A sprig of lavender she plucked,
Which in my pinafore she tucked.
"The sweetest flower of memory, this,"
Said she. Then bent again to kiss
My cheek; and to this hour,
I see her face in every flower.

BEGONIAS AND FUCHSIAS
Butchart Gardens/British Columbia, Canada
Dennis Frates/Oregon Scenics

HANDMADE HEIRLOOM

◆ ◆ ◆

HANDMADE PINCUSHIONS. Crafted by Mary Skarmeas. Jerry Koser Photography.

PINCUSHIONS
Mary Skarmeas

My dear mother, who was never without a needle and thread, had some very interesting places to secure her needles as she went about her daily tasks. The bib of her ever-present apron was always adorned with a few safety pins or a needle with a length of thread, ready to repair a seam, take up a hem, or mend a tear. The side hems of our kitchen curtains were another hiding place for needles and pins put down in the rush of daily life. I remember being a small child and waking one night to find my mother in her favorite rocking chair by the kitchen stove, a basket full of socks in her lap and her needle and thread working steadily. In a family of thirteen children, mending and darning were ongoing tasks.

Eventually, however, all of Mama's many

needles and pins did find their way to a home base—the pincushion. Mama had several, but the one that intrigued me the most was a plump, round pillow that sat atop an old cookie tin. Inside the tin were hundreds of buttons waiting for a second life. The pillow was made with a piece of blue velvet salvaged from a lovely old coat Mama had saved from her own childhood, and it was trimmed with lace and satin bows. It has been said that the past becomes more vivid to us through the cherished small objects of daily life than through the great events and artifacts of history. Such a cherished object is my mother's handmade pincushion, the image of which evokes in me a rush of memories of a time and a place far removed from modern life.

The humble pincushion has a colorful history. As long as there have been needles, there have been pincushions. Even before metal pins and needles were made, small slivers of bone from animals and fish, as well as sharp, thin thorns, were used as needles to decorate clothing. Because of their sharpness and fragility, these needles had to be protected. Some Native Americans made soft cases of animal skins to protect and house their bone needles. Later, in other cultures, women safeguarded their sewing tools in small tubes made from silver or ivory. Pincushions as we know them today evolved after mass-produced metal pins became available. The first pincushions were made of linen, satin, or canvas and were embellished with embroidery. Small ones were made to hang from purses on decorative cord. In the days when needlework and sewing were a part of almost every woman's day, pincushions were a necessary accessory.

In the eighteenth century, pincushions were imprinted with political slogans or designed to commemorate a historical event. Everything from a family wedding to the death of a national hero was at one time or another immortalized on a pincushion. Pincushions went on to become a popular decorative item in the nineteenth century, made for wall hanging or for table display. Both fads came and went, however, and the pincushion returned to its utilitarian role by the side of the seamstress.

Today, most pincushions are mass produced, and with sewing less a part of everyday life, they are often relegated to a shelf or a drawer out of view. Yet pincushions are easy to make, and the craft is experiencing something of a revival. The basics are easy enough for anyone—two pieces of fabric sewn together and stuffed tightly to create a pillow. The rest is all decoration and imagination. Entire books devoted to the art of the pincushion discuss how to use baskets and tins, lace and ribbon, embroidery or cross-stitch to turn the ordinary pincushion into something worth bringing out into view. A handmade pincushion is a wonderful craft, something that can be completed in an afternoon, but used and enjoyed for a lifetime.

My mother's special pincushion was both a necessity and a bit of an indulgence. Blue velvet did not hold needles any better than did plain muslin, but she took pride in her needlework, took pleasure in this tiny touch of luxury in a life with little time for such things. I wish I had that blue velvet pincushion on its button tin today; what a perfect remembrance of Mama it would be. Looking at it would remind me of the mother who worked so hard to care for us, who sat up nights sewing by the stove, but also of the mother who always tried to bring a touch of color and fun to our day-to-day lives and who always found some way to make each one of her children feel special.

Mary Skarmeas lives in Danvers, Massachusetts, and has recently earned her bachelor's degree in English at Suffolk University. Mother of four and grandmother of three, Mary loves all crafts, especially knitting.

GRANDMOTHER'S TREASURES

Luceille Carey Seigfred

Her favorite books, and a Bible well read,
A wicker basket with scissors and thread,
Packets of needles, a thimble worn thin,
A frayed velvet cushion with many a pin,
Old-fashioned buttons, ribbons and lace,
A few little keepsakes tucked into place,
An album of pictures she cherishes so,
And a bundle of letters tied with a bow;
Grandmother's treasures—all waiting there,
And a faded kimono thrown over her chair.

Grandma is sleeping, just resting awhile.
She soon will awaken, and we'll see her smile
As into her treasures her dear hands will go
To dream once again of the sweet long ago.

MEMORY is the diary
that we all carry
about with us.

—Oscar Wilde

Devotions FROM THE Heart

Pamela Kennedy

. . . I call to remembrance the unfeigned faith that is in thee,
which dwelt first in thy grandmother Lois, and thy mother Eunice;
and I am persuaded that in thee also.

2 Timothy 1:5

THREADS OF FAITH

When my children were young I tucked each into bed at night with hugs and kisses and a tickle or two. As they snuggled into the security of quilts and coverlets, we always took a few minutes to say prayers together. It was a precious time when we knit up all the loose ends of the day and presented them to God, certain that He would know what to do about each one. As the children grew, these bedtime prayers became springboards for questions about weightier matters, morals, ethics, and biblical views of current-day issues.

I recall having similar discussions with my own mother as she sat on the edge of my bed late at night. We probably never solved any great problems, but I remember the security it gave me to know I could talk about anything with Mother. In her wisdom, she didn't always provide an answer, but consistently pushed me toward God, who did have the answers I sought.

Not too long ago, I overheard my mother-in-law, deep in conversation with my daughter. They were pondering the greatness of a God who could manage all the business of the universe and still have time to care for one young girl's concerns.

In each of these situations, the thread of faith was woven from one generation to the next by mothers and grandmothers who cherished and trusted the truth of God. What a valuable heritage we pass along as we pick up the thread ourselves and stitch it into the fabric of our families. Sometimes that thread is a brightly shining glimmer of hope to an anxious grandchild. Another time it may mark the way for a confused adolescent. Once in a while, the strong fiber of faith becomes a veritable life line, helping a child to escape from desperate circumstances or fears.

Just as Paul cited in Timothy's case, the fabric of faith is not self-made. It is painstakingly, lovingly woven together by those who take the time to teach us. As grandmothers and mothers, we have the God-given privilege of taking part in this process. We too can help knit together generations with the precious threads of faith.

O Lord, help me take the time to gently weave
strong threads of faith into the lives of my children and grandchildren.
AMEN.

Grannie

Vernon Scannell

I stayed with her when I was six then went
To live elsewhere when I was eight years old.
For ages I remembered her faint scent
Of lavender, the way she'd never scold
No matter what I'd done, and most of all
The way her smile seemed, somehow, to enfold
My whole world like a warm, protective shawl.

I knew that I was safe when she was near.
She was so tall, so wide, so large, she would
Stand mountainous between me and my fear;
Yet oh, so gentle, and she understood
Every hope and dream I ever had.
She praised me lavishly when I was good,
But never punished me when I was bad.

Years later war broke out and I became
A soldier and was wounded while in France.
Back home in hospital, still very lame,
I realized suddenly that circumstance
Had brought me close to that small town where she
Was living still. And so I seized the chance
To write and ask if she could visit me.

She came. And I still vividly recall
The shock that I received when she appeared
That dark, cold day. Huge Grannie was so small!
A tiny, frail, old lady. It was weird.
She hobbled through the ward to where I lay
And drew quite close and, hesitating, peered.
And then she smiled; and love lit up the day.

TO AN UNBORN GRANDCHILD

Isla Paschal Richardson

Across the waiting hours I send my love
To welcome you. We should have much in common,
You and I, holding so dear the one whose life links ours.
Let us be friends.

This world is vastly interesting to which you come,
And gloriously worthwhile its span of life.
Think clearly, and look up. Life can be fine and strong.
I shall not lecture nor admonish, nor prod you with ambition.
One thing, just this one thing I ask of you:
Help me to pay a debt. You are the only one who can.
(Ah, it will be years and years—and even then
You may not ever know the depth of love she holds for you,
The one whom you call Mother!)

Do this for me:
From that first heaven-born moment
When she looks into your dewy, wondering eyes,
And dimpled, rose-leaf fingers cling to hers,
Please bring into her life
As much joy and sunshine
As she has given mine.

Ideals' Family Recipes

Favorite Recipes from the Ideals Family of Readers

Editor's Note: Please send us your best-loved recipes! Mail a typed copy of the recipe along with your name, address, and phone number to Ideals magazine, ATTN: Recipes, P.O. Box 305300, Nashville, Tennessee 37230. *We will pay $10 for each recipe used. Recipes cannot be returned.*

GRANDMA'S CREAM CHEESE COOKIES

Preheat oven to 350° F. In a medium bowl, sift together 2 cups all-purpose flour and ½ teaspoon salt; set aside. In a large bowl, cream 1 cup butter or margarine and one 8-ounce package cream cheese with 1 cup granulated sugar until light and fluffy. Add 2 eggs and 2 teaspoons vanilla; stir well. Add flour mixture; stir well. Stir in one 11½-ounce package milk chocolate chips and 1 cup chopped walnuts. Drop dough by rounded teaspoons onto greased baking sheet. Bake 10 to 12 minutes. Cool on wire rack. Makes about 3 dozen cookies.

Gayle Lockwood Fell
Corona, California

MOLASSES COOKIES

Preheat oven to 350° F. In a medium bowl, sift together 2½ cups sifted cake flour, 1 teaspoon baking soda, 1 teaspoon ground cinnamon, 1 teaspoon ground ginger, ¼ teaspoon ground cloves, and ¼ teaspoon salt; set aside. In a large bowl, cream ½ cup softened butter or shortening with ½ cup granulated sugar until light and fluffy. Add 1 egg and ½ cup molasses; stir well. Add the flour mixture in 3 parts, alternating with ½ cup buttermilk, stirring well after each addition. Stir in ½ cup chopped raisins. Drop dough by rounded teaspoons onto greased baking sheet. Bake 8 to 12 minutes. Cool on wire rack. Makes about 40 two-inch cookies.

Mrs. Joseph Hermetz
Detroit, Michigan

Deluxe Oatmeal Cookies

Preheat oven to 350° F. In a medium bowl, sift together 2 cups all-purpose flour, 1 teaspoon baking powder, ½ teaspoon baking soda, and ½ teaspoon salt; set aside. In a medium bowl, combine ½ cup shredded coconut, ½ cup semisweet chocolate chips, ½ cup chopped walnuts, ½ cup raisins, and 2 cups quick oats; set aside.

In a large bowl, cream 1 cup shortening with 1 cup granulated sugar and 1 cup light-brown sugar until light and fluffy. Add 3 eggs, one at a time, beating well after each addition. Add 1 teaspoon vanilla extract; stir well. Add flour mixture a little at a time; mix well. Stir in oats mixture. Shape a heaping tablespoon of dough into a ball without packing it. Place balls 2 inches apart on an ungreased baking sheet. Bake 12 to 15 minutes. Do not overbake. Makes about 3½ dozen cookies.

Dorothy E. Shumate
Grand Rapids, Michigan

Marshmallow Fudge Cookies

Preheat oven to 400° F. In a medium bowl, sift together 3 cups all-purpose flour, 1 teaspoon baking soda, and ½ teaspoon salt. Stir in ⅔ cup cocoa; set aside. In a large bowl, cream 1 cup softened margarine with 1 cup granulated sugar and ½ cup firmly packed light-brown sugar until light and fluffy. Add 2 eggs and 1 teaspoon vanilla; stir well. Add flour mixture; stir well. Place 2 miniature marshmallows inside a rounded teaspoon of dough; seal well. Roll in granulated sugar and place on greased baking sheet. Repeat for remaining dough. Bake 5 to 7 minutes until cookies crack. Cool on pan 2 minutes; remove to wire rack. Makes about 3½ dozen cookies.

Norma Schmatt
Cedar Rapids, Iowa

Surprise Cookies

Preheat oven to 350° F. In a medium bowl, sift together 1 cup all-purpose flour, ½ teaspoon baking soda, ¼ teaspoon salt, and ¼ teaspoon baking powder; set aside. In a large bowl, cream ½ cup softened butter with ½ cup granulated sugar and ½ cup firmly packed light-brown sugar until light and fluffy. Add 1 egg and 1 teaspoon vanilla; stir well. Add flour mixture; stir well. Stir in ½ cup quick oats, 1 cup wheat flake cereal, ¾ cup angel flake coconut, ¾ cup coarsely chopped pecans, and ¾ cup milk-chocolate-covered raisins. Drop dough by teaspoons onto a greased baking sheet, flatten lightly with fork dipped in cold milk. Bake 10 minutes. Cool on wire rack. Makes approximately 3½ dozen cookies.

Margaret Schroeder
Saint Charles, Missouri

BOYHOOD DAYS

Nathaniel Parker Willis

There's something in a noble boy,
A brave, freehearted, careless one,
With his unchecked, unbidden joy,
His dread of books and love of fun,
And in his clear and ready smile,
Unshaded by a thought of guile,
And unrepressed by sadness—
Which brings me to my childhood back,
As if I trod its very track,
And felt its very gladness.

And yet, it is not in his play,
When every trace of thought is lost,
And not when you would call him gay,
That his bright presence thrills me most:
His shout may ring upon the hill,
His voice be echoed in the hall,
His merry laugh like music trill,
And I in sadness hear it all—
For, like the wrinkles on my brow,
I scarcely notice such things now—

But when, amid the earnest game,
He stops, as if he music heard,
And, heedless of his shouted name
As of the carol of a bird,
Stands gazing on the empty air,

As if some dream were passing there—
'Tis then that on his face I look,
His beautiful but thoughtful face,
And, like a long-forgotten book,
Its sweet familiar meanings trace—

Remembering a thousand things
Which passed me on those golden wings,
Which time has fettered now;
Things that came o'er me with a thrill,
And left me silent, sad, and still,
And threw upon my brow
A holier and a gentler cast,
That was too innocent to last.

'Tis strange how thoughts upon a child
Will, like a presence, sometimes press,
And when his pulse is beating wild,
And life itself is in excess—
When foot and hand, and ear and eye,
Are all with ardor straining high—
How in his heart will spring
A feeling whose mysterious thrall
Is stronger, sweeter far than all!
And on its silent wing,
How, with the clouds, he'll float away,
As wandering and as lost as they!

My Mother's Rocking Chair

Marcella Drennan Malarky

I loved my mother's rocking chair,
　　So cheery and so bright.
'Twas small and stout and painted red;
　　It was my chief delight.

The seat was deep, the back was round;
　　It fit you, oh, so snug.
I loved to rock in Mother's arms;
　　She'd hold me tight and hug
Me, oh, so close up to her heart
　　To make my fears depart.

I'd love to see once more, my dear,
　　That well-loved rocking chair,
To be a child in Mother's arms,
　　To feel the comfort there.
Her kitchen and the old blue clock,
　　The winding wooden stair;
Oh, memory dear has painted clear
　　A picture, oh, so fair,
Of Mother and her kitchen and
　　The little rocking chair.

A Little Boy

Iris W. Bray

All the sweetness and the mirth
　　He gathered up from round the earth—
A star of hope to wish upon,
　　A breath of faith, a ray of sun,

A shrug, a boast, a grin so wide,
　　An ounce of curious thoughts and pride,
A pocketful of fun and jest,
　　A pound of inquisitiveness,

A dash of vigor, pep, and vim,
　　Then just for fun, a stroke of whim,
A store of faith, a world of trust,
　　A little "kicking up of dust,"

An ardent love of crawling things,
　　An eagerness that laughs and sings,
Mischievousness that means no harm,
　　A burst of captivating charm.

To all these things He measured love
　　With His own blessing from above
And planted them in fertile soil
　　Where mortals live and dream and toil.

He breathed a soul and wept a prayer;
　　His tender seed He blessed with care.
It grew to be a thing of joy—
　　This gift of God, a little boy!

THROUGH MY WINDOW

Pamela Kennedy

Art by Ron Adair

FUND-RAISING FOLLIES

If you are a mother with children who are old enough to join an organization or go to school, then you have been baptized in the fires of fund-raising. Whether you help on the committee to dream up great revenue-producing ideas, serve with the hearty souls who administer the fund-raiser, or end up hauling around your offspring door to door, you know firsthand the trials and tribulations of raising money.

We have three children and have lived in many different parts of the country; and I can assure you, fund-raising is not a regional phenomenon. It goes on everywhere. The products may change from place to place (my kids sold *huli-huli* chicken in Hawaii and designer wrapping paper in Virginia), but the techniques and time involved remain constant.

Really smart fund-raisers begin their campaigns by gathering all the children together at a time when their parents are not there, like soccer practice or during lunch at school. They first tell the children the sad tale of how they will be deprived of some wonderful opportunity or piece of equipment because there isn't enough money available. When the kids are convinced of their dire situation, the fund-raising person holds out the only hope in town: the fund-raiser! He regales his potential sales force with tales of abundant resources, rediscovered hope, and, best of all, prizes! Eager hands reach for the sales brochures while visions of compact disc players and bicycles dance in youthful heads.

This is the point at which mothers usually get involved. When those newly inspired salespeople burst in the front door with plans of making the Fortune 500 selling greeting cards, mini-pizzas, cinnamon bread, or Christmas wreaths, guess who gets the task of escorting them from customer to customer? My experience tells me that after about a dozen doors, the thrill of door-to-door sales begins to wane. Even if everyone buys something, the salesman's dreams inevitably collide with reality.

"Mom, do you know how many of these I have to sell to earn enough points to get even the Genuine Space Flashlight?!!"

"Of course I do. And what's more, the selling is just the beginning. You have to keep records, tally your sales, collect the money, assemble your orders, and then deliver them." I'm a firm believer in reality.

Of course, that's when the little shoulders begin to sag, the bottom lip trembles, the innocent eyes widen, and my resolve starts to erode just the tiniest bit. The next day, Dad takes the brochure to work and leaves it out in a conspicuous place "in case anyone wants to order something." What he's banking on is that everyone walking through the office is also a parent with a kid who is now or has in the past participated in a fund-raiser. It's something you never forget!

By the deadline date most kids haven't sold half of what they anticipated and are in grave danger of losing out on the wonderful opportunity or piece of equipment the funds were intended to purchase. They are convinced they will be the only soccer team without shorts, the only fourth grade that doesn't go to science camp, the only school lacking CD-ROM drives on their computers.

This is when that extra freezer you picked up at the garage sale comes in handy. We have had as many as sixteen loaves of Auntie Belinda's Cinnamon Bread and a dozen of Auturo's Peerless Pepperoni Pizzas in our freezer at one time. And one Christmas many of our dear friends received stationery supplies, wrapped in designer paper—all leftovers from the school sale.

Recently, I've noticed a decline in the popularity of fund-raisers which require the kids to sell products door to door. I applaud this trend; however, it hasn't stopped the money-making efforts of most schools and organizations, just redirected them. We now have the new, improved, one-time extravaganza fund-raiser—usually a carnival, parking-lot sale, or book fair. I actually prefer these because they only cause intense involvement for one or two days and leave you with an empty freezer.

Last year my daughter's school had a carnival, and I was in charge of the sponge toss booth. It was great fun charging the children to toss soaking sponges at their teachers. And most parents, probably recalling their own school days, seemed eager to finance their children's soggy target practice. We made a healthy, if damp, profit.

Book fairs are perhaps a more civilized way to raise funds. I enjoy working at them because I get to sit in the library and watch all the other mothers get dragged around from display to display by their excited little readers. Book fairs have success written all over them because parents hardly ever say "no" to a child who wants to buy reading material, even when they realize Junior's new-found interest in literature is taking a bite out of next month's grocery money. Book fairs really rake in the cash.

This year, my daughter's school is taking a new approach. Parents have the option of either participating in a fund-raiser or sending in a check as a donation. Some may find this offensive, but I think it shows a good grasp of economic reality. In fact, I was just getting out my checkbook when the doorbell rang. There on my front porch stood a diminutive entrepreneur dressed in a Sunbeam Girl outfit.

"Would you like to buy a can of caramel corn so my troop can go to camp?" she asked.

I looked down the walkway and spied a mother half-concealed by the hedge.

I sighed and smiled at the little Sunbeam Girl on the porch. "Sure, honey, I'll take two." She brightened, turned, and waved two fingers at her mother, who responded with a "thumbs up" from behind the hedge. Oh well, I already had my checkbook out; and besides, I think her bottom lip was starting to tremble.

Pamela Kennedy is a freelance writer of short stories, articles, essays, and children's books. Wife of a naval officer and mother of three children, she has made her home on both U.S. coasts and currently resides in Honolulu, Hawaii. She draws her material from her own experiences and memories, adding highlights from her imagination to enhance the story.

Butterfly Kisses

Margaret Rorke

Butterfly kisses! I almost forgot!
Really that would have been sad.
Watching a mother a-hugging her tot
Posted a mem'ry I had.
Long, long ago, I was given that treat—
One that a child shouldn't miss.
Often I stood on the toes of my feet
Just for a butterfly kiss.

Butterfly kiss—don't you know how it's done?
Gather a cheek to your eye.
Brush it with "winkers" you flutter in fun.
Soon it will giggle and cry,

"Oh, how it tickles! Let's do it again!
Do it to sister like this!
Tell me, though, Mother, just where and just when
You saw a butterfly kiss?"

Mothers don't see them, and yet mothers know,
Know that it has to be true
Just 'cause the mother they loved told them so.
That's how I know it. Don't you?
Maybe a butterfly settled on Eve
Back when all Eden was bliss,
Showing her how; so all tykes might receive
Joys of a butterfly kiss.

Within My Heart

Hilda Butler Farr

Oh, how I love to reminisce
As mothers always do,
Relive again within my heart
The childhood days of you.

I picture you upon the floor
With cars and blocks and trains,
The little wooden soldiers too,
And every kind of plane.

The day you started off to school
It was a big event.

I see you now, your rosy face,
As down the street you went.

You liked to skate and ride a bike
Then added to the list
The love of books and radio;
There wasn't much you missed.

So much has happened through the years;
It's now a memory.
The little boy has disappeared,
Except of course to me.

51

BREAKFAST IN BED. Mary Cassatt, artist (1845–1926). The Huntington Library, San Marino, California. Superstock.

My Son-in-Law

Isla Paschal Richardson

I hold my baby in my arms
And rock her to sleep.
Somewhere, perhaps in far-off lands,
You laugh and romp and play,
Or you may be one of her playmates
Up the street.

Too swiftly fly these first sweet years
When she is mine.
Weariness can have no claim upon me
When I am serving her. And yet—
Just when the day has come
When we have found companionship—
Then you will come.
Forgive me if I pray that you will not come
Too soon.
The years fly by so fast—so fast!

Be good to her.
Her joyous heart was made for happiness.
Be gentle, too,
Lest she should miss the comfort and the tenderness
Of mother-love.
My eager lips will tremble with so many things I want to say;
Of little things that made her glad—
Of things she loves.

But you will smile and think you know her better than I—
Than I, her mother.
My lips will silent be
Save for the prayers they murmur for her happiness—and you.
And I will smile
That I may cast no shadow on her shining path
With you.

God grant that you may keep your life both clean and strong
Until you come for her.
That you may learn—what few have learned—
The things that make a woman happiest.
Oh, do not let the thirst for wealth crowd out
The little joys that you could have
Together.
She will not miss the wealth so much
But she would miss your goodbye kiss—
Should you forget.

Be good to her,
And make her happy. Then I shall be content
With memories.
These first sweet years, you know, are mine,
Are mine!

A SLICE OF LIFE

Edgar A. Guest

ROSES

When God first viewed the rose He'd made,
  He smiled, and thought it passing fair;
Upon the bloom His hands He laid,
  And gently blessed each petal there.

He summoned in His artists then
  And bade them paint, as ne'er before,
Each petal, so that earthly men
  Might love the rose for evermore.

With heavenly brushes they began,
    And one with red limned every leaf,
To signify the love of man;
    The first rose, white, betokened grief;
"My rose shall deck the bride," one said
    And so in pink he dipped his brush,
"And it shall smile beside the dead
    To typify the faded blush."

And then they came unto His throne
    And laid the roses at His feet,
The crimson bud, the bloom full blown,
    Filling the air with fragrance sweet.

"Well done, well done!" the Master spake;
    "Hence forth the rose shall bloom on earth:
One fairer blossom I will make,"
    And then a little babe had birth.

On earth a loving mother lay
    Within a rose-decked room and smiled,
But from the blossoms turned away
    To gently kiss her little child,
And then she murmured soft and low,
    "For beauty, here, a mother seeks.
None but the Master made, I know,
    The roses in a baby's cheeks."

Edgar A. Guest began his illustrious career in 1895 at the age of fourteen when his work first appeared in the Detroit Free Press. *His column was syndicated in over three hundred newspapers, and he became known as "The Poet of the People."*

Patrick McRae is an artist who lives in the Milwaukee, Wisconsin, area. He has created nostalgic artwork for Ideals *for more than a decade, and his favorite models are his wife and three children.*

A Time of Joy

Elizabeth Symon

The buttercups and dandelions,
    And daisies, well-known names,
We gathered in the garden then
    For my young daughter's games.

"Let's see if you like butter,"
    She would ask me with a grin
As she held glossy petals up
    To glow beneath my chin.
"You do, Mummy, you do, just look!
    You do!" she'd cry with glee.
The gold reflection of the flower
    Was there, we would agree.

And with a wealth of little flowers
    She'd make a daisy chain
By threading all the tiny stems
    In, out, and in again.

When this ploy tired, she then would take
    One daisy from the lot,
And picking petals one by one,
    Play "Loves Me, Loves Me Not!"

And if the dandelions had bloomed
    And they were past their prime,
She'd joy in blowing their seed "clocks"
    To help her tell the time.
"A one, a two, a four," she'd puff.
    "I think I missed out three,
Or should that one be five o'clock?
    Can you help count with me?"

Oh, springtimes past and long ago,
    A time of fun and flowers,
I wish I could call back again
    Those happy, carefree hours!

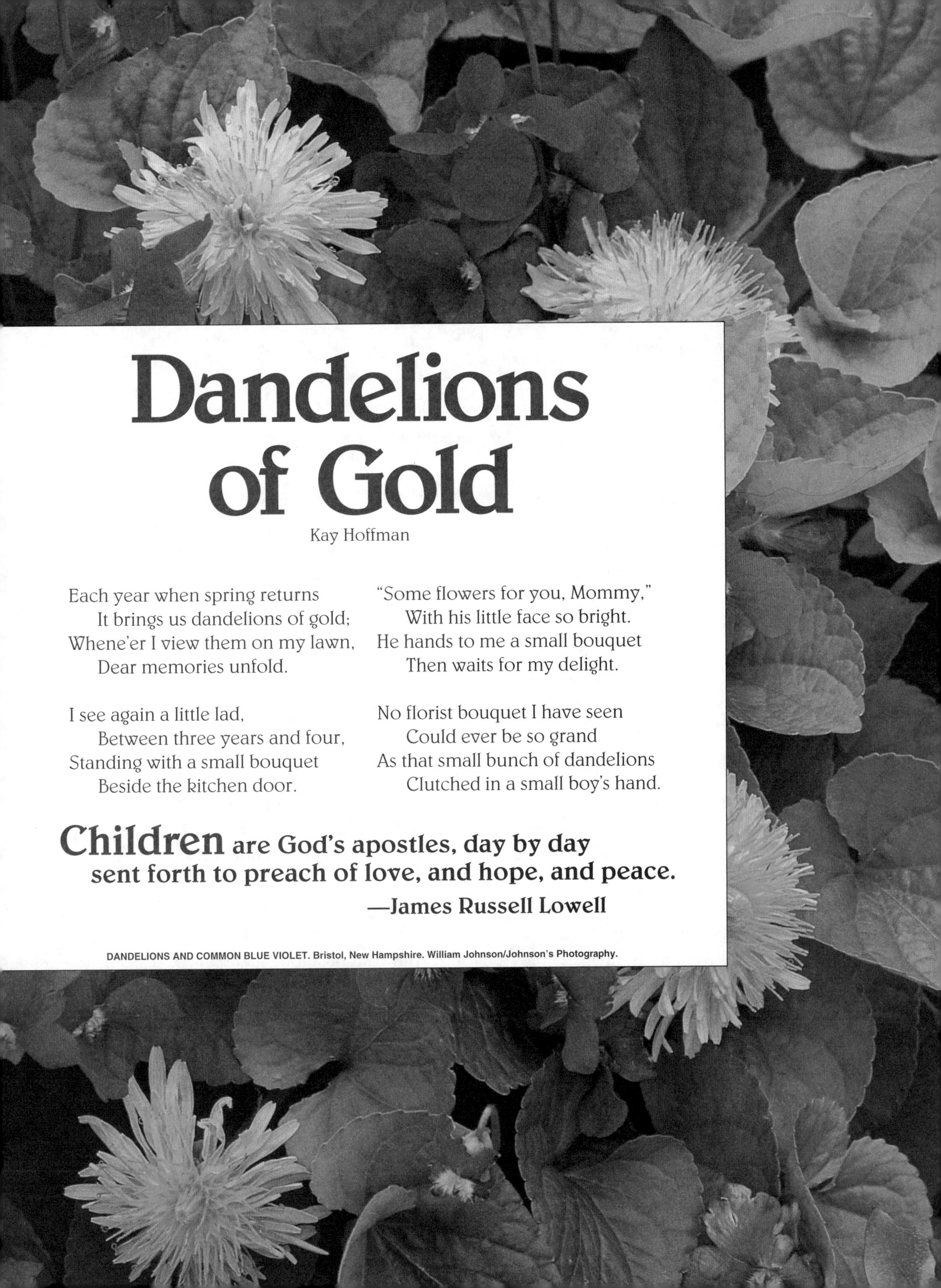

Dandelions of Gold

Kay Hoffman

Each year when spring returns
   It brings us dandelions of gold;
Whene'er I view them on my lawn,
   Dear memories unfold.

I see again a little lad,
   Between three years and four,
Standing with a small bouquet
   Beside the kitchen door.

"Some flowers for you, Mommy,"
   With his little face so bright.
He hands to me a small bouquet
   Then waits for my delight.

No florist bouquet I have seen
   Could ever be so grand
As that small bunch of dandelions
   Clutched in a small boy's hand.

Children are God's apostles, day by day
  sent forth to preach of love, and hope, and peace.
               —James Russell Lowell

DANDELIONS AND COMMON BLUE VIOLET. Bristol, New Hampshire. William Johnson/Johnson's Photography.

Mama's Homegrown Love

Lon Myruski

Within my breast lie woven
For heart and soul to share,
Dear sentiments of Mama—
She loves, she dreams, she cares.
She nurtured farm and family
With hoe and gentle hugs;
We grew along together
On Mama's homegrown love.

On Sundays in the winter
Around our parlor's fire,
We'd share warm family feelings
That Mama would inspire.
Then in our country kitchen
She'd cook the dinner up,
So generously flavored
With Mama's homegrown love.

Those sultry nights of summer
Out on our front-porch swing
Where Mama'd read me stories
Then serve homemade ice cream.
I'd get a tuck at bedtime;
A kiss and tender touch—
A sweeter second helping
Of Mama's homegrown love.

Now from my field of mem'ries
Wave flourishing bouquets;
For my heart is a garden
Abloom with bygone days.
In reveries I walk there
To reap grand harvests of
My cherished thoughts of childhood
And Mama's homegrown love.

OUR HERITAGE

LETTER TO MRS. BIXBY

Abraham Lincoln

November 21, 1864

Dear Madam:

I have been shown in the files of the War Department a statement of the Adjutant General of Massachusetts that you are the mother of five sons who have died gloriously on the field of battle. I feel how weak and fruitless must be any words of mine which should attempt to beguile you from the grief of a loss so overwhelming. But I cannot refrain from tendering to you the consolation that may be found in the thanks of the Republic that they died to save. I pray that the Heavenly Father may assuage the anguish of your bereavement, and leave you only the cherished memory of the loved and lost, and the solemn pride that must be yours to have laid so costly a sacrifice upon the altar of freedom.

Yours very sincerely and respectfully,

Abraham Lincoln

ABOUT THE AUTHOR

Although he was born, in 1809, into a poor, illiterate family in Hardin County, Kentucky, Abraham Lincoln became one of the most important men in American history. Forty days after his inauguration in March of 1860, the shot at Fort Sumter began the bloodiest war in American history. Lincoln delivered a moving cemetery-dedication speech on November 19, 1863, in Gettysburg, Pennsylvania, voicing his belief in the union of America and his respect for the soldiers, like Mrs. Bixby's sons, who had died to defend that belief. Five days after General Lee surrendered at Appomattox, Lincoln was shot by John Wilkes Booth while attending a performance at Ford's Theatre. Abraham Lincoln died the next morning, April 15, 1865. A black-clad railroad car named the "Lonesome Train" carried Lincoln's body more than 1,700 miles to Springfield, Illinois, where he was laid to rest.

—Tara E. Lynn

On a Seventeenth Birthday

Anne P. L. Field

Today my tall, broad-shouldered lad,
　　With such a grave, protective mien,
I watched with eyes grown strangely sad,
　　Though proud these mother-eyes had been,
For brave and bonny seventeen
　　Is not a saddening sight to see;
Yet I have lost, long years between,
　　My little boy that used to be!

How well remembered and how glad
   That hour when happier than a queen
A rosy infant son I had,
   When all the singing world was green;
With what deep gratitude serene
   I welcomed my maternity.
He was the sweetest ever seen
   My little boy that used to be!

I see him now in velvet clad
   And just a trifle vain, I ween,
Showing his new suit to his dad
   As male birds their fine feathers preen.
His curls had such a golden sheen,
   And by his crib on bended knee
I'd pray God's love from harm would screen
   My little boy that used to be!

ENVOY
O son upon whose strength I lean,
   Be very patient, dear, with me;
For mothers miss with anguish keen
   The little boy that used to be!

CORNER

PERFUME BOTTLES
by Melissa A. Chronister

COLLECTOR'S

On my most recent birthday, my mother gave me a delicate, hand-blown, glass perfume bottle. The bottle design was inspired by Victorian styles, a personal favorite, and created by a local artisan. As I held the bottle up to the sunlight, my memory transported me back to my childhood when I received my first bottle of perfume.

I was seven when my grandmother presented me with perfume in a bottle shaped like a dropped ice-cream cone. "Splat," as I nicknamed it, was the first in a long series of miniature perfume bottles Grandma selected for me during the time she sold cosmetics. I was thrilled to get my own bottle of perfume since I had always loved watching Grandma perform her morning ritual of applying perfume. From the several glittering glass bottles on her dresser, she'd select one and dab the liquid on her wrists and throat in just the right spots. On those rare occasions when she would dab a little on my wrist too, I felt so grown up.

All of the items in my initial collection of perfume bottles were gifts, but I remember my first purchase. I found a simple, pale blue atomizer at a nearby flea market. On my way home, remembering that blue was my mother's favorite color, I realized she would adore the beautiful perfume bottle even more than I would. Cradled in its satin-lined box with ornate pewter hinges, the atomizer provided a delightful Mother's Day surprise. As a reminder of our times together, I later placed a similar atomizer in my row of perfume bottles against the window.

My fascination with perfume bottles grows with each addition to my collection. With so many unique shapes and colors, I never tire of wandering through the dusty glassware shelves of antique shops, one of my favorite venues for great bottles. I found my most important bottle, however, at an outdoor tag sale in my own neighborhood. That Saturday morning as I looked over the items for sale, I found a dirty, blue glass bottle on a lower shelf. The shape was one I'd seen before; so even though it was in poor condition, I purchased the bottle—and at a bargain price. A good soak in warm water revealed a woman's silhouette on the front and a signature on the bottom—René Lalique, a famous French designer from the Art Nouveau period of the early 1900s. I was thrilled to have such an old piece to add to my collection.

Additions to my collection are as frequent as my pocketbook will allow. My most precious collectible is a special edition of "Gardenia," released by Molinelle in 1930. Resembling an inverted pyramid with a gold lid, the French perfume bottle is a treasured wedding gift from my husband. "Gardenia" stands at the center of my collection, surrounded by my other perfume bottles, each of which represents the treasured memory of a special moment in my life. And every chance I have, I add another memory.

COMMON SCENTS

If you would like to start a collection of perfume bottles, here are some tips to help you get started:

HISTORY

• Perfume bottles have been around for thousands of years; before the invention of indoor plumbing, perfume was primarily used to mask unpleasant body odors.

• In the 18th century, tiny scent bottles were often worn on a chain; "scent" was a strong perfume containing ammonia to aid in recovery of fainting spells.

• Around 1907, manufacturers began to create bottles specifically for one fragrance; previously, perfumes had been sold in generic containers.

• The value of a perfume bottle increases with age, rarity, unique features, and condition. Highly desirable are the original labels, cap, packaging, and contents.

• Bottles fewer than one hundred years old usually cost up to $25.00; whereas older, rare items may sell for up to $200.00 or more.

FOCUSING COLLECTIONS

Due to the wide variety of perfume bottles, you may wish to focus your collection. Some ways to do so include:

• The work of a particular glassworks manufacturer, such as Henry William Stiegel

• Colored bottles in jewel tones, such as amber, ruby, sapphire, emerald, or amethyst

• Famous designers' glassware, such as French Lalique or Gallé

• Decorative stoppers made of gold, silver, cloisonné, or semi-precious stones

• Miniature "scent" bottles, some even as small as one inch long

• Antiques dated from a particular era, such as French bottles from the 1920s

• Victorian, Art Nouveau, or Art Deco styles

• Figural bottles resembling automobiles, boots, bull horns, or insects

ANTIQUE PERFUME BOTTLES. Spencer Jones/FPG International.

• Different package designs of your favorite fragrance

CARE AND DISPLAY

• Chips or cracks in a bottle, even if they have been repaired or altered with resin, will decrease the value of the item.

• Soak stained or dirty bottles in a mild solution of lukewarm water and soap or ammonia. Use harsher chemicals or a brush with caution to avoid scratching; *never* mix chemicals.

• Perfume bottles make beautiful displays when arranged on shelves in front of a window or artificial light. Group your pieces by color, shape, or size.

A Wish for My Children

Evangeline Paterson

On this doorstep I stand
year after year
and watch you leaving

and think: May you not
skin your knees. May you
not catch your fingers
in car doors. May
your hearts not break.

May tide and weather
wait for your coming

and may you grow strong
to break
all webs of my weaving.

ROSE BUSH ON EASY STREET
Nantucket Island, Massachusetts
William Johnson
Johnson's Photography

My Favorite Mother's Day Memory

Personal Stories of Treasured Memories from the Ideals Family of Readers

One Special Mother

"Let me tie a ribbon in your hair," Grandma Reed would say as she helped me prepare for Sunday School. Sundays were always busy with church, family dinners, visiting, and helping Grandma at the store across from the church we attended. Since my mother died when I was three years old, my wonderful grandma devoted her senior years to raising me and my four siblings. She struggled to give each child quality time and lots of love.

Grandma gathered us children around a small table in the back room of the store for nourishing food and cold milk. "I'll help you, dear," Grandma would say as she placed a big spoonful of delicious macaroni and cheese on my plate.

Mother's Days spent with Grandma were always happy times, and each one of us made a simple gift for our substitute mom. "Oh, sweetheart, thank you, it is a lovely gift," Grandmother expressed to each child for the remembrance. She hugged us often and said, "I love you."

No one could ever take the place of Mom, but Grandma sure was a close second. We didn't have everything we wanted, but we were certainly rich in love, hand-me-downs, faith in God, and memories.

Phyllis M. Peters
Three Rivers, Michigan

A Bouquet of Love

Early on Mother's Day morning when I was a little girl, I would go out into our large backyard and pick a handful of sweetly scented purple violets for Mother. Or at other times on Mom's special day, I would opt for an assorted array of tulips from the flower garden in front of our house. But if the lilac bush next to our front porch bloomed early enough, I would surprise Mom with a perfumed bouquet of double-whites. After carefully choosing the flowers, I'd go into the house, find a Mason or jelly jar, put the flowers in it (with water, of course), and set the jar of beauties on the kitchen table for Mom to discover.

Years later, Mom told me the nicest gift of all on Mother's Day was the gift of surprise. She never knew what kind of flowers would adorn the kitchen table on Mother's Day morning!

Patricia A. Owen
Newark, New York

Seaside Memories

It seems like yesterday that my daughter and I were lazily enjoying the late afternoon peace that had gradually settled over the beach one day during our summer vacation. The rest of the family had gone inside; the clamor and squeals of joyous children splashing nearby had subsided as they too had taken leave of the sand and sea.

My young daughter and I, lost in our own world, were building a sand castle, complete with a moat. Gradually, the incoming tide crept closer, filling the moat once, twice, until finally the next wave demolished our architectural wonder, walls and all. We laughed and turned our attention to collecting seashells.

The air sharpened as the sun dropped in the west behind us. It was time to go inside, but we continued to cling to the spell of the beach at late afternoon. We found a perfect, unbroken shell that had to be the smallest ever to survive the sea and the trampling of little feet.

On the beach that afternoon, I felt a happiness that is almost indescribable. It was so unexpected—the simple chatter with my little daughter, the lengthening shadows, the quiet of the beach, and the utter stillness of the sea as it paused between the waves crashing ashore. This picture is not in my photo album; this "snapshot" of those precious moments is forever imprinted on my heart.

My small daughter grew up, and last summer I joined her and her family during their beach vacation. My two grandsons and I had great fun as we spent one late afternoon building sand castles and searching for seashells long after everyone else had gone inside.

Since my daughter and her family and I live far apart, I didn't see them again until they visited me this year. When they arrived, the first thing the boys noticed was an object on my desk. "Grandma," they squealed, "here's one of the seashells we found at the beach last summer!" My secret was out. "I couldn't throw it away," I replied, "and every time I see it, I think of you and remember what fun we had on the beach that day." Their jaws dropped, and a look of wonder briefly crossed their faces. At that instant, I felt a new bond between us, linked by a happy memory that we shared.

As for me, I have another memory as well, and it revolves around a beach, a bucket and shovel, and a small child of yesteryear.

Margaret Wheeler
Manassas, Virginia

Nineteen Roses

On April 22, 1965, our son, Jim, came home from Iowa State College bringing his mother a beautiful bouquet of nineteen red roses with a card saying, "Nineteen roses for nineteen years as my fabulous mother." It was Jim's nineteenth birthday.

From one proud dad and proud husband,

Verne O. Phelps
Edina, Minnesota

Two Small Hands

After experiencing forty-three happy Mother's Days, it is hard to pick one gift or one day that stands out above all the rest. But tucked away among my memories is a faded, green card and on it a faded, pink crepe paper carnation.

She was seven years old. She came home from school hiding something behind her back. "Don't peek," she admonished, so I knew she had something for me.

We got up early on Sunday to get ready for Sunday School. It was raining. She put on her raincoat and went out the back door before I could say, "Don't go out in the rain." But she came back quickly and put a handmade, rain-soaked Mother's Day card in my hand. She had hidden it in the bushes in the backyard.

I still have that rain-soaked card, faded now of its colors, but enriched with love from two small hands of one who loved her mother.

Ann Welborn
Mabelvale, Arkansas

Editor's Note: Do you have a special holiday or seasonal memory that you'd like to share with the Ideals *family of readers? We'd love to read it! Send your typed memory to:*

My Favorite Memory
c/o Editorial Department
Ideals Magazine
535 Metroplex Drive, Suite 250
Nashville, Tennessee 37211

A Mother's Prayer

Margaret Ellen Jacob Rice

Seated at the kitchen table,
    Alone and late at night,
Her head is bowed in reverence,
    Her hands are folded tight.

The prayers she whispers softly
    Are filled with words of love,
Requesting for her children
    God's help from up above.

"Dear Jesus watch and keep them
    And guide their steps each day,
Set angels all around each one,
    And help them on their way.

"Dear Lord, I know it's in Your will,
    And I am much obliged
That You will shape and carefully tend
    Each aspect of their lives."

God's loving eyes gaze down at her;
    He hears, He knows, He cares.
For she has touched the heart of God
    With her tender mother's prayer.

LEGENDARY AMERICANS

PATRICIA A. PINGRY

MARY MAPES DODGE

"On a bright December morning long ago, two thinly clad children were kneeling upon the bank of a frozen canal in Holland." So begins *Hans Brinker; or, The Silver Skates*, a children's novel published in 1865. In the story, Hans Brinker, fifteen, and his sister Gretel, age twelve, can't skate very far or very well on their crude, homemade wooden skates described as "clumsy pieces of wood narrowed and smoothed at their lower edge, and pierced

with holes, through which were threaded strings of rawhide." Overcoming many odds and enduring several family tragedies, Gretel wins a contest for a pair of girl's silver skates; and the family is restored.

Upon publication, *Hans Brinker* became an immediate best seller. Critics hailed it as a travel book for its accurate depiction of Holland scenery and Dutch life. Parents loved it for its themes of endurance, self-sacrifice, and triumph. But children loved it because the characters behaved as real children with all their fears, disappointments, and challenges which they somehow overcame.

When *Hans Brinker* was published, the author, Mary Mapes Dodge, a young widow with two young sons to support, lived at her parents' estate in New Jersey. At the time, she had gotten no farther from home than New York City; yet the themes of the novel came straight from her life and experiences; and her ability to communicate to children as their comrade and friend came from an innate respect for her own children. Such a love and understanding of children led to Dodge's success as the most innovative editor and writer of children's literature in her time.

Mary Elizabeth Mapes was born in New York City, January 26, 1831, to Sophia and James Jay Mapes. In 1850 Mr. Mapes relied on a young lawyer named William Dodge to help him buy a new family home in Waverly, New Jersey. When Dodge came to the Mapes home to meet the family and complete the deal, the thirty-two-year old lawyer fell in love with the Mapeses' nineteen-year-old daughter Mary Elizabeth, nicknamed Lizzie. The two were married a year later and moved to New York City to live with Dodge's family. Two sons were born to the couple; and life was, apparently, peaceful. In fact, some of Lizzie's later short stories seem to be partly autobiographical and, if so, indicate that she had a busy and happy married life.

William Dodge, however, became involved in James Mapes's complicated financial dealings—not always straightforward—with friends and associates. Mr. Mapes had borrowed money from Dodge to finance his New Jersey estate, then subsequently mortgaged and remortgaged the home. By 1857 Mr. Mapes's financial structure began crumbling, putting financial and emotional stress upon Dodge. An additional burden also presented itself when the Dodges' younger son was diagnosed with a serious disease that threatened him with death or, at best, a life of invalidism. On October 28, 1858, William Dodge went out for a walk and never returned. His body was later recovered, and the cause of death was listed as drowning.

Mary Mapes Dodge moved to the Mapeses' estate in New Jersey and resolved to "take up her life again in the old spirit of rejoicing; to rear and educate her boys as their father would have done; to do a man's work with the persistent application and faithfulness of a man, to gain a man's pay, yet to leave herself freedom and freshness to enter into all her children's interests and pursuits as their comrade and friend."

Dodge was totally committed to providing for her children. She flew kites with them, skated with them, and swam with them; she went on long hikes with them and collected various butterfly or botanical specimens. When faced with providing for her boys financially, she first experimented with writing and editing magazines for adults; but she was quick to observe that fewer people were writing for children, and the market was more open. This was the impetus for *Hans Brinker* and its predecessor, *The Irvington Stories,* a collection of stories about boys. Thus, when the position of editor for a children's magazine was offered, Mary Mapes Dodge accepted the position for which she had, unknowingly, been prepared.

As successful as *Hans Brinker* was (and still is with translations in print throughout the world), Mary Mapes Dodge, during her lifetime, was better known as the editor of what has often been called "the best of all children's magazines"—*St. Nicholas*. Dodge once described her magazine as a "pleasure ground" for children, and she intended that it should indeed be such a pleasure from cover to cover.

Dodge was offered the position of editor in 1873 with complete control for this new children's magazine to be published by Scribner and Company. In selecting the name of the periodical, Dodge said, "the name should belong to no time or nationality, and that it should belong inalienably to all children." In an effort to give her young readers the type of magazine they wanted to read, she polled her audience. In one column, she informed them how seriously she took their advice; but she also made it plain that she would not compromise *her* standards. She told the story of a boy who hid the book he was reading every time his father passed and advised that one should never read what one was ashamed of: "Bad reading is a dangerous poison; and I, for one, would like to see the poisoners— that is, the men who furnish it—punished like any other murderers; yes, and more, for it's worse to kill the soul than to kill the body." From these precepts, *St. Nicholas* published writers such as Louisa May Alcott, Mark Twain, Rudyard Kipling, and Jack London; it gave the gift of quality literature to children for more than thirty years.

Embedded in *Hans Brinker* is a fable about a little Dutch boy who on his way home sees a leak in the dike. At once, he understands the danger and sticks his finger in the hole. The boy is delighted that he has stopped the leak, but then he begins to feel cold, fear, numbness, pain. In spite of his discomfort and fear that he might not survive the night, he vows that he will remain steadfast until morning. Along with his rescue, the young boy receives praise and honor from his country.

In her life, Mary Mapes Dodge exhibited the same courage and endurance as that young boy. Buffeted by personal tragedies, including the death of her younger son, Dodge remained steadfast until her death in 1905 in her commitment to her own personal and professional standards. In so doing, she set the standards of excellence in children's literature: presenting honest children in realistic situations performing with courage, dignity, and selfless heroism. For her contribution, Mary Mapes Dodge receives the grateful thanks and accolades from children of all ages who have read her stories, and from children all over the world who have yet to meet Hans Brinker.

A Golden Memory

Johanna Ter Wee

Long years have past, yet there remains
A memory forged with golden chains
That ever binds me to the past—
A childhood memory made to last.
For constantly throughout the years
Remembrance comes of banished fears
When lamps were dimmed and prayers were said
And Mother tucked me into bed.

A Parent's Prayer

Leonard Withington

At this hushed hour, when all my children sleep,
Here in Thy presence, gracious God, I kneel;
And, while the tears of gratitude I weep,
Would pour the prayer which gratitude must feel.
Parental love! Oh, set Thy holy seal
On these soft hearts which Thou to me hath sent;
Repel temptation, guard their better weal;
Be Thy pure spirit to their frailty lent,
And lead them in the path their infant Saviour went.

BEDTIME. Carlton Alfred Smith, artist (1853–1946). Christie's, London. Superstock.

BITS & PIECES

In the eyes of its mother every beetle is a gazelle.
—*African Proverb*

No gift to your mother can ever equal
her gift to you—life.
—*Author Unknown*

A mother understands
what a child does not say.
—*Jewish Proverb*

A mother is God's deputy on earth.
—*Rachel L. Varnhagen*

Thank you, God,
  For pretending not to notice that one of
  Your angels is missing and for guiding
    her to me.
  You must have known how much I
    would need her, so
  You turned your head for a minute
    and allowed her to slip away to me.
  Sometimes I wonder what special
    name you had for her.
  I call her "Mother."
            —*Bernice Maddux*

An ounce of mother is worth
  a pound of clergy.
        —*Spanish Proverb*

Mother is food; she is love;
  she is warmth; she is earth.
  To be loved by her means to be
  alive, to be rooted, to be at home.
          —*Erich Fromm*

Motherhood is the greatest
  privilege of life.
      —*May R. Coker*

Gail Roth

Music

Author Unknown

I've heard the woodwinds and the trees
A duet play, and thund'ring seas
In deep-toned symphony I've heard,
And flute-note of a mother bird.
Heard too a sweet exotic strain
Played in a forest by the rain,
Accompanied by mountain stream,
Exquisite music—yet these seem
To fade as I turn in the path
To home, and hear a baby laugh.

FOR THE CHILDREN

from *Catalogue*
Rosalie Moore

Cats sleep **fat** and walk thin.
Cats, when they sleep, slump;
When they wake,
 s t r e t c h and begin
Over, pulling their ribs in.

Cats walk thin. . . .Cats sleep **fat**.
They spread out comfort

underneath them

Like a good mat,
 As if they picked the place
 And then sat;

You walk around one as if he were the City Hall

After that.

OLD HOUSES

Homer D'Lettuso

There is comfort in old houses,
Like a mother's arm, or a friend's kind words.
There is joy in time-scarred timbers,
In slated roofs and weathered boards.
   (I am one with an old house;
   I am one with its pains and joys.
   An old house shared the travail of my mother.
   An old house shared my baby toys.)

Old houses have a blessed look,
That is one with God's great plan.
Old houses have a tenderness,
From the baby's crawl to the stride of the man.
   (I am one with an old house,
   I am one with its kind embrace.
   An old house shared my mother's love.
   An old house knew my mother's lovely face.)

THE OLD HOMESTEAD
Mills, Nova Scotia
Gene Ahrens Photography

WILD MORNING-GLORY. Everglades National Park, Florida. Stan Osolinski/FPG International.

Morning-Glories

Linnea H. Bodman

When morning-glories wake at dawn,
    They smooth their wrinkled skirts and yawn.
Then, wide awake, they seem to say,
    "Good morning! Have a lovely day!"

But when the sun has climbed up high
    And starts its journey down the sky;
Their eyelids droop, and they collapse,
    All curled up for their beauty naps.

There is no time
Like spring
When life's alive
In everything.

    —Christina Georgina
      Rossetti

Morning-glory is
  the best name.
It always refreshes
  me to see it.

    —Henry David
      Thoreau

Upon the Hill

George R. Kossik

The splendor of the summer sun
    Shone bright above the hill,
And all the verdant vale below
    Lay beautiful and still.

The songs of birds with sweetness filled
    The summer-scented air,
And I alone upon the hill
    Saw God was everywhere.

Readers' Forum
Meet Our Ideals Readers and Their Families

The editors at Ideals are looking for well-written, nostalgic reminiscences, especially about life on the farm. If you have a memory of the treasured days of yesteryear on the farm, send your typed manuscript to: NOSTALGIC REMINISCENCES, C/O EDITORIAL DEPARTMENT, IDEALS MAGAZINE, P.O. BOX 305300, NASHVILLE, TENNESSEE 37230.

DIANE FOSSETT from Piedmont, South Carolina, sent us this photograph of her grandsons Jarrett Morris and Cody Knight. Two-year-old Jarrett (left) is the son of Chris and Dina Morris. Cody, five months younger than his cousin, is the son of Jeffrey and Donna Knight. The idea for the picture originated when Diane's husband bought the boys cowboy hats at a local flea market. After several attempts involving lots of wiggling, crying, and falling off the steps, the cousins sat still long enough for Diane to catch them on film. "The shot came back so great I just had to send it in," Diane said.

BILL AND BILLIE BUCKLES of Alva, Oklahoma, share this picture of their granddaughter, Darcy Dean, when she was four years old. Darcy is enjoying the annual carnival hosted by her mother's employer. As far as her proud grandparents are concerned, Darcy's smile sets any room aglow. She is quite a talkative young lady, says "Nana" Billie. Daughter of Rusty and Tamara Dean of Willow Park, Texas, Darcy is also the beaming older sister of recent-arrival Devon.

THANK YOU Diane Fossett and Bill and Billie Buckles for sharing with *Ideals*. We hope to hear from other readers who would like to share photos and stories with the *Ideals* family. Please include a self-addressed, stamped envelope if you would like the photos returned. Keep your original photographs for safekeeping and send duplicate photos along with your name, address, and telephone number to:

READERS' FORUM
IDEALS PUBLICATIONS INC.
P.O. BOX 305300
NASHVILLE, TENNESSEE 37230

Publisher, Patricia A. Pingry
Editor, Lisa C. Ragan
Copy Editor, Michelle Prater Burke
Electronic Prepress Manager,
Tina Wells Davenport
Editorial Assistant, Tara E. Lynn
Editorial Intern, Melissa A. Chronister
Contributing Editors,
Lansing Christman, Deana Deck,
Pamela Kennedy, Patrick McRae,
Mary Skarmeas, Nancy Skarmeas

ACKNOWLEDGMENTS

An excerpt from CATALOGUE by Rosalie Moore, copyright © 1940 The New Yorker Magazine, Inc. Reprinted by permission. MY SON-IN-LAW and TO AN UNBORN GRANDCHILD from *MY HEART WAKETH* by Isla Paschal Richardson, copyright © 1947 by Bruce Humphries, Inc. Used by permission of Branden Publishing, Boston. GRANNIE from *LOVE SHOUTS AND WHISPERS* by Vernon Scannell. Reprinted by permission of Hutchinson's Children's and Random House UK Ltd. A NEW NOTE from *THE ROUND OF THE YEAR* by Patience Strong, copyright © 1948. Reprinted by permission of Rupert Crew Limited. Our sincere thanks to the following authors whom we were unable to contact: Marie Hunter Dawson for APART, Homer D'Lettuso for OLD HOUSES, Henry Clay Hall for WHO DOES NOT LOVE TRUE POETRY, Marcella Drennan Malarky for MY MOTHER'S ROCKING CHAIR, and Evangeline Paterson for A WISH FOR MY CHILDREN.

When Spring's Brief Days Are Spent

Gail Brook Burket

The milk-white blossoms of the spring
Have but a fleeting day;
Then in a cloud of petal snow
They lightly drift away.

But branches bright with growing leaves
Or leaves in burnished prime
Or boughs aglow with autumn gold
Are lovely all the time.

Black branches tipped with scarlet seeds
And wreathed with silver snow
Attain a beauty more intense
Than other seasons know.

The springtide glory soon is gone,
But watch it fade content;
More glory follows, if we see,
When spring's brief days are spent.